Simply Ice Cream

Easy Recipes for the Ice Cream Lover

Chef Sterling Smith

Simply Ice Cream

ISBN-13: **978-1515105596**
ISBN-10:1515105598

DEDICATION

Many thanks to my daughters, Ava and Eden, who inspire me every day to do great things – to cook, teach, experiment, learn, and love. Many thanks to my wife, who challenges me, supports me, and loves me.

This book was cooked while picking strawberries and cherries from a farm in Orange County, NY. Beautiful fruit, beautiful setting, beautiful pickers – Ava and Eden … Thank you!

Chef tested, kid approved, all natural recipes.

No chemicals, additives, or coloring required.

The best ice cream is made from simple ingredients (cream, eggs, fresh fruit) and simple techniques.

All recipes were tested in my home kitchen, using a Noxon 700 ice cream machine from Italy.

The Noxon 700 takes between 35 - 40 minutes to make a batch of ice cream.

In this work-horse machine, I have produced thousands of 2 ½ quart batches over the past 10 years.

CONTENTS

1
VANILLA SKY ICE CREAM

Yields 3 generous quarts

Ingredients:

8 c. Heavy Cream

1 c. Whole Milk

2 c. Sugar

Zest of ½ Lemon

1½ tsp. Vanilla Extract

12 Egg Yolks

In a heavy pot, bring heavy cream and milk to a simmer (just below a boil). Add lemon zest and vanilla. Turn off the heat.

In a bowl, gently whisk egg yolks and sugar, until the mixture turns a pale yellow color. Pour two or three ounces of the hot cream into the yolk mixture and stir well. (That is technically called tempering.)

Pour the yolk mixture into the hot cream mixture and stir well.

Turn back on to a medium heat and continually stir the mixture, scraping the sides and bottom until the mixture slightly thickens. It should coat the back of a spoon. (A Chef's tip: You should be able to run your finger over the back of the covered spoon. The mixture should stay in place and not run together. The space formed by your finger should remain. This is called Napant.) Caution: do not let mixture boil.

Strain the mixture through a fine sieve or Chinois strainer and chill the mixture. (Placing the bowl containing the mixture in an ice bath is a great and fast way to chill the mixture.)

Freeze in ice cream maker according to the manufacturer's specifications.

Enjoy, or freeze in an air tight container.

2
CHOCOLATE DELIGHT

Yield: 2 quarts

Ingredients:

4 c. Whole Milk

4 c. Heavy Cream

3 c. Sugar

9 Yolks

8 oz. Semi-Sweet Chocolate- chopped

4 tbs. Cocoa Powder

Pinch Sea Salt

Heat cream, milk and half the sugar in a heavy bottomed pot. Bring it to a gentle simmer. Add the chocolate and let it melt, gently whisking to incorporate. Add the cocoa powder and mix well. Once it is mixed, take it off the heat and let it sit.

In a bowl add the yolks and half of the sugar. Whisk until mixture turns a light pale color. Pour a few ounces of the hot cream mixture into the egg mixture and stir well. Turn

3

on to a medium heat and continually stir the mixture, scraping the sides and bottom until the mixture slightly thickens. It should coat the back of a spoon. Caution: Do not let mixture boil.

Strain through a sieve or Chinois, and chill. Note: An ice bath is a great and fast way to chill the mixture.

Freeze in ice cream maker according to the manufacturer's specifications.

Enjoy, or freeze in an air tight container.

3
BERRY STRAWBERRY ICE CREAM
A quick no egg ice cream

Yield: 3 quarts

Ingredients:

3 pt. Strawberries (fresh or frozen)

4 c. Sugar

Zest of 1 Orange

6 c. Heavy Cream

3 c. Whole Milk

1 tsp. Lemon Juice

In a bowl, place the cleaned strawberries, 1 cup sugar, orange zest and lemon juice. Let it sit for 45 minutes.

In a heavy bottomed pot, add the cream, milk and the remaining sugar. Bring the mixture to a simmer. Stir well, by scraping sides and bottom of the pot so mixture doesn't scorch. Mixture should thicken until it coats the back of the spoon. Add the strawberry mixture and simmer 1 to 2 minutes.

Chill mixture in an ice bath. (Place the bowl in a bowl of ice water.)

Freeze in ice cream maker according to the manufacturer's specifications.

Enjoy, or freeze in an air tight container.

4
GO GREEN – HEAVENLY PISTACHIO ICE CREAM

Yield: 2 generous quarts

Ingredients:

4 c. Half and Half

3 c. Whole Milk

9 Egg Yolks

2 c. Green Pistachios

2 ½ c. Sugar

1 tsp. Pistachio Extract

Soak the pistachios in warm water for 10 minutes and drain. Set it aside.

In a heavy bottomed pot, add the cream, milk and 1 ½ cups of sugar. Bring to a simmer.

In a bowl, add the yolks and 1 cup sugar. Whisk until mixture turns a pale yellow color.

Add a ¼ cup of the hot cream mixture to the yolk mixture and mix well.

Next, add the yolk mixture to the hot cream mixture. Simmer, continually stirring and scraping the sides and bottom of pan until the mixture thickens enough to coat the back of a spoon. Stir in the pistachio extract.

Strain the mixture through a sieve or Chinois and chill. An ice bath is a great and fast method to chill the mixture.

Add the pistachios (whole) and freeze in an ice cream machine to manufacturer's specifications. Alternatively, for a smoother ice cream, puree the pistachios in the strained liquid and then place in the ice cream machine.

Enjoy, or freeze in an air tight container.

5
NUTTY BUTTER PECAN ICE CREAM

Yield: 4 quarts

Ingredients:

8 c. Heavy Cream

3 c. Half and Half

14 Egg Yolks

2 c. Pecans (toasted)

3 ½ c. Sugar

2 tsp. Vanilla Extract

3 tsp. Bourbon

2 tbs. Butter

Pinch of Sea Salt

Mix the pecans, 1 cup sugar, butter and a pinch of sea salt in a cake or pie pan. Bake at 325 deg. for 10 minutes. Let cool.

In a heavy bottomed pan, add the heavy cream, half and half, and 2 cups of sugar. Bring to a simmer, stirring well.

In a bowl, add the yolks and remaining ½ cup of sugar. Whisk well, until the mixture turns a pale yellow color.

Add a couple of ounces of the hot liquid to the yolk mixture and mix well. Then, add the yolk mixture to the hot cream. Add bourbon and vanilla extract. Return to medium heat, continually stir the mixture, scraping the sides and bottom until it slightly thickens. Caution: Do not boil the mixture.

Strain the cream mixture, add the pecan mixture and chill. An ice bath is a fast and great way to chill the mixture.

Freeze in ice cream maker according to the manufacturer's specifications.

Enjoy, or freeze in an air tight container.

6
MINTY FRESH CHOCOLATE CHIP ICE CREAM

Yield: 2 quarts

Ingredients:

2 c. Half and Half

2 c. Whole Milk

6 Egg Yolks

1 ½ c. Sugar

1 ½ tsp. Mint Extract

¾ c. Semi-sweet Mini Chocolate Chips

½ tsp. Vanilla Extract

Pinch of Salt

In a heavy bottomed pot, add milk, half and half and 1 cup of sugar. Bring to a gentle simmer.

In a bowl, add the yolks and ½ cup of sugar. Whisk until it reaches a pale yellow color. Add ¼ c. of the hot milk mixture and stir well. Add the yolk mixture to the hot cream and, on medium heat, continue stirring the mixture, scraping the sides and bottom until the mixture thickens enough to coat the back of the spoon. Don't boil.

Strain mixture add the vanilla and mint extracts. Chill mixture. An ice bath is an easy method for chilling the mixture. Next, add the chocolate chips.

Freeze in ice cream maker according to the manufacturer's specifications.

Enjoy, or freeze in an air tight container.

7
BANANA BROWN SUGAR ICE CREAM

Yield: 2 generous quarts

Ingredients:

4 Ripe Bananas

2 c. Brown Sugar

1 tsp. Vanilla Extract

½ tsp. Sea Salt

8 c. Whole Milk

12 Egg Yolks

Peel the bananas and place them on a cookie sheet. Cover the bananas with ¼ cup of brown sugar and sprinkle with sea salt. Roast the bananas in a 350 deg. oven for 30 minutes. Let cool.

In a heavy bottomed pot, heat the milk until it reaches a gentle boil. Remove the milk from the heat.

In a separate bowl, combine remaining sugar with the egg yolks and whisk for 4 minutes. Take 4 oz. of the hot milk and whisk it into the yolk mixture.

Add the egg mixture to the pot of milk. Return the mixture to a medium heat, continually stirring and scraping down the sides and the bottom of the pot until it slightly thickens (170 deg.). Add the vanilla extract.

Place the mixture in an ice bath to cool.

Take the roasted bananas and rough chop them. Add them to the ice cream mixture.

Freeze in ice cream maker according to the manufacturer's specifications.

Enjoy, or freeze in an air tight container.

8
DRUNKEN RAISIN ICE CREAM

Yield: 2 generous quarts

Ingredients:

4 c. Heavy Cream

4 c. Whole Milk

2 ½ c. Dark Raisins

1 tsp. Vanilla Extract

1 c. Dark Rum

3 c. Sugar

12 Egg Yolks

Soak the raisins in the rum until soft and plump, about 20 minutes. Set aside the drunk raisins for later use.

Place the cream, milk, 2 cups of sugar and vanilla extract in a heavy bottomed pot. Heat the mixture until it reaches a gentle boil. Remove the pot from the heat.

In a bowl, add the egg yolks and remaining sugar. Whisk the mixture until it turns a pale yellow color. Take 4oz. of the hot cream mixture and add it to the yolk mixture. Mix well.

Add the egg mixture to the pot of milk. Return the mixture to a medium heat, continually stirring and scraping down the sides and the bottom of the pot until it slightly thickens (170 deg). Do not let the mixture boil.

Place the mixture in an ice bath and let chill.

Next, add the drunken raisins to the mixture.

Freeze in ice cream maker according to the manufacturer's specifications.

Enjoy, or freeze in an air tight container.

9

CHEF STERLING'S TIPS & TRICKS FOR GREAT ICE CREAM MAKING

1. When heating the cream or milk mixture, use a thermometer.

2. The temperature of the mixture, when cooking, should be between 165/170 deg. – the perfect temperature to thicken without boiling.

3. For a quick way to make chocolate ice cream, use chocolate milk instead of the chocolate and cocoa powder mixture.

4. Frozen strawberries are okay.

5. Creaming (whisking) the yolks and sugar until they become a pale yellow color, gives the ice cream great texture and flavor.

6. Use a heavy bottomed pot so as to not burn or scramble the eggs in the mixture.

7. Straining the mixture in a Chinois or fine strainer helps remove egg particles and any zest or impurities.

10

ABOUT THE AUTHOR

Born and raised on a farm in the mountains of West Virginia, Chef Sterling was aware at an early age of the essential value of freshness and sustainability. Where other children were playing hide and seek, Sterling was scouring the countryside for wild delicacies, such as ramps and morels. Natural childhood exploration turned into a culinary passion for Sterling.

One of his fondest memories as a child was making ice cream in a hand turned ice cream maker - adding ice and salt and a lot of elbow grease. The fresh milk from the cows on the farm was an added bonus.

Chef Sterling was formally trained at The Culinary Institute of America, in Hyde Park, New York. He perfected his craft and fed his passion while working at some of New York's top restaurants.

As the proud father of two aspiring chefs, Chef Sterling enjoys making fresh pasta and ice cream with his daughters Ava and Eden.